Surviving A Broken Relationship

No longer a victim, but a victor.

by
Ruth King

Bloomington, IN  Milton Keynes, UK

 authorHOUSE™

AuthorHouse™
1663 Liberty Drive, Suite 200
Bloomington, IN 47403
www.authorhouse.com
Phone: 1-800-839-8640

AuthorHouse™ UK Ltd.
500 Avebury Boulevard
Central Milton Keynes, MK9 2BE
www.authorhouse.co.uk
Phone: 08001974150

First published by AuthorHouse 5/22/2006

ISBN: 1-4259-3391-2 (sc)

*Printed in the United States of America
Bloomington, Indiana*

This book is printed on acid-free paper.

Contact the author at ruthking0202@yahoo.com.

This book is dedicated to the loving and fond memories of my Mom & Dad, The late William King and the late Arlene King with love. Through their training and love of God, I became a Christian.

Table of Contents

Introduction

The contents in this book deals with the hurt and pain brought on by a broken relationship, especially broken relationships of couples whether by marriage, or merely dating or a very strong friendship will be hurtful. We all know it is not easy to say good bye to a significant other. In any relationship, a bonding takes place. An oneness of spirit sprouts in intimate relationships. In reality the two become a part of each other in many aspects.

It is the strength and bonding of relationships that make it hard to be without that significant other. When you have shared intimacy with someone, very detailed and specific things are shared between the two and each of the parties becomes a strength or backbone for one another. When the strength and backbone suddenly disappears, one will experience a number of feeling, and the heartbreak as well as emotional shock. Most of us who have experienced this type of relationship and then have the relationship brake apart, know the depth of experiences you feel when you are faced with this break-up. Suddenly the joys and shared events in life are over and you are left alone to face the emptiness and pain.

This book will shed light on how this type of break-up can make you or break you. It also shares the important decisions that one make, will be some of the most important decisions one could make under such circumstances.

Not only are you faced with not having a companion and friend, but you are forced to deal with everything solo. Loneliness ultimately becomes an ugly enemy that could leave one feeling hopeless.

When a person feels violated by a breech of paper or verbal contract it is a very devastating feeling. It could take sometimes weeks, months and even years to heal and know how to move on in life. This book will entail many of the different emotions, traumas, and setbacks of broken relationships, and how to bounce back from low to high, and how to get a handle on this monster of emotions. Even those who have been left alone through the death of a loved one will be helped by reading this book, because the grieving processes for both types of broken relationships are pretty much the same.

Many have given up on life and the hope of having any other relationship. Some people have let depression rule and take preeminence in their lives, and ultimately allow pain and rejection rule their lives. This book sheds light on how broken relationships causes people, because of misfortune go through mild to extreme difficulties.

During my recent breakup, I felt overwhelmed many times and I began to go to several phases of emotional issues, which ultimately had severe impacts on my life as a Christian. In other words, I did not allow what I had learned throughout the years to work. My experiences and emotional pain took first place in my life and my life as a Christian suffered, because depression would not allow me to trust God and place all of my problems in God's hand. My problems and pain became my God subconsciously. The experience also affected my relationships with others, because basically people could not really relate to what I was going through, but the only one that really could relate and understand it all was God.

I did not feel that I could get the real help from God, because I had prayed and prayed as well as others, but still the pain and suffering would not go away, but I realize now that I handled everything wrong. I did not turn my back on God but I was just there.

This book shares how I went from being the victim to being the victor/conqueror. Through the course of time and prayers prayed, I began to feel on my way to wholeness. Being whole involves a feeling of restoration of heart, mind and body and soul. It's a feeling of forgiveness. Understanding the reason people may offend you or forsake you really makes it easy to forgive them. Once you understand that a committed person would not have violated the covenant between you, unless there was some pertinent reason. You will find many answers to unanswered questions as you read through the book and healing will take place as you understand the "why".

Chapter One
"Dealing with the Hurt"

Being in a relationship and have it come apart at the seams can be very devastating. It hurts so much, because of the bonding that had taken place and having shared so many happy times together throughout the relationship.

Many people, whether Christians or non-Christians often feel trapped in a haven of pain and depression and isolated after a break-up. One may become so angry, until bitterness and resentment sets in. Depression is almost always included with any broken relationship, especially those relationships that were very intimate and those that have been in the relationship for many years. Depression leads people to shut down on life and you become withdrawn from others, in particular from any form of potential new relationships. In some situations, vulnerability many times causes people to rush into the arms of others to fulfill the loneliness and ease the ache of the break-up.

Being rejected by someone you love and cherish may leave you feeling desponded and hurt and even confused. Whether your relationship was through rejection or through losing someone through death, the grief process is about the same. Many of the feelings that one experience after losing a significant other are natural and will ultimately take time for healing and restoration to take place.

Questions are natural in humans after a lost. Such questions as, why me?, What did I do to deserve this?, I thought we loved each other?, Why was I rejected?, Are my physical features not attractive any more?, Is it my age?, Have I gained too much weight?, Did I become boring?, Was the thrill gone away?, Was I exciting to his interest etc? These are some of the things that may come to mind after experiencing a break-up.

Regardless of the answers to the many questions that may hunt you, we must face our pain and find ways to heal. Seeking healthy ways to heal is most vital to your well being and those closest to you. It is very important for the hurting and rejected persons not to take the blame for the break-up. Even the most loving couples still have areas that can be improved upon, so no relationship is perfect. With time and age people change, things change, our looks change, because God made our bodies to change with time. At certain ages, we do not desire some of the things we desired years before, but the real word in any relationship is **<u>Commitment</u>**. Surely, changes in people should not have one to throw away the commitment of their relationship. Some relationships have taken years to cultivate and grow, and then to throw it away overnight is not wise, but is a very selfish act. The question anyone should ask is, should I stop investing in this relationship that I have spent years trying to build? Remember, it takes two people to want the relationship. You can want to keep the relationship, but if the other party does not want to stay and make it work, you can't do it alone. Count your lost and move on!!

Proverbs 5:17-20 "Let them be only thine own, and not strangers with thee, let thy fountain be blessed and rejoice with the wife of thy youth, let her be as the loving hind and pleasant roe; let her breasts satisfy thee at all times; and be thou, ravished always with her love, and why wilt thou, my son, be ravished with a strange woman, and embrace the bosom of a stranger."

Have we forgotten the vows that were exchanged at the altar that goes like this: will you love, honor and cherish until death do you part, in sickness, in health, for better, for worst, for richer, for poorer etc.? **"COMMITMENT"**

WHAT HAPPENED TO THIS TYPE OF COMMITMENT?

Regardless of whether there were a friend-to-friend breakup, or husband and wife break-up, one thing is certain, and that is, it hurts!!! You not only have to deal with the hurt but you also must deal with the many things that you are faced with. Some of the things you will wonder about is: how can I believe in myself again, will there be another relationship and if so will I have to face this music again, or how can I avoid going down this road again, how and what am I to do now after being left and kicked to the curb? After

3

all you are quickly thrown back into the single life, if you were married.

When I was rejected after 30 years plus of marriage, some of those questions came to my mind. I sought comfort from God, and people, but I did not find comfort. The pain did not leave, it was still there. It felt as if I had to go through the process and pain of it all. Many times I looked for a listening ear to understand the pain, and I looked for a compassionate heart, but realistically, I wanted someone to help me to stop hurting, in actuality the bible had all the answers that I needed.

God have all the strength, comfort, direction and biblical help I needed for my situation. I believe I wanted more than that. I wanted something and someone tangible, someone that I could see and hear to tell me it would get better. Through all of it, I finally sought God's help, and accepted his way of getting me through the grief and despondency that I was going through.

Don't get me wrong, I spent many nights crying and praying to God, but instead of me leaving my burdens with God in prayer, I took the problems back and tried to figure it out and rationalize everything. The Lord let me know that, "all things work together for good, to them that love the Lord, and to them who are the called according to his purpose." Romans 8:28

Until I learned to trust and depend on God, I continued seeking help and advice from people; the truth is that everyone has a different opinion, and many can't relate to your pain, because they have not experienced your pain, and even those who have had some similar situations may have seen things in a different way, and maybe chose not to disclose their deep feelings of hurt, pain and rejection.

One analogy of a broken relationship is death. Death breaks up a relationship between people, just as a break-up of a couple or friends. Divorce or calling it quits is the death of a covenant or an agreement, and it must be grieved and healed the same as an actual death. We all may know and have experienced a separation, and the pain that goes along with it. Certainly losing a loved one through death will cause some of this pain.

In time, I learned that this separation and the end of a 30-year-marriage was the same pain that many experience everyday when one have lost a loved one.

We are allowed to grieve with any loss, but we must grieve healthy, and not let a broken relationship tear us down. In other words, not to give up on life and people, but most of all, not give up on God. When someone gets hurt physically, either by falling or by a car accident, it really hurts initially but there is always a better tomorrow. Time heals all wounds. There is a guaranteed healing with time.

There is a bright future awaiting each of us; for life in itself is a gift from God. God will revive you, and give you hope and joy, and he will take away the hurt and give you a bright and prosperous tomorrow, if you let him. He will restore everything you lost.

Let go, and let God begin to mend your broken heart. So what we were rejected, but guess what, there will be someone to accept and love you, even better than you were ever loved.

"Believe and you will receive, if you doubt, you will be without." "And Jesus answering said unto them, have faith in God. For verily I say unto you, that whosoever shall say unto this mountain, be thou removed, and be thou cast into the sea; and shall not doubt in his heart, but shall believe that those things which he saith shall come to pass; he shall have whatsoever he saith. Therefore, I say unto you, what things so ever ye desire, when ye pray, believe that ye receive them and ye shall have them." Mark 11:22-24

Remember, God cares for you, no matter what you have been through. He wants to take away the pain and hurt from your heart. Let him give you a renewed mind and spirit, rest in his loving arms. He is a healer and he is a restorer and a repairer of the breech. Let him restore your peace, joy, happiness and zest for life.

Let God restore you to wholeness, and allow God to send you someone that will treat you the way you need to be treated. Many times God want to give us someone better; He knows that many have made mistakes in their choices for a partner, and he knows whether that person brings you down or is just not for you. You must receive God's healing, so you will be whole for the next person God sends you. God is touched by the feelings of your infirmities (weaknesses).

One thing that will keep you locked up in pain is un-forgiveness. If you carry anger bitterness, resentment and un-forgiveness towards the person that hurt you, you are giving that person power over you. This power will keep you locked up in misery and pain. Not only will your prayers be hindered, but you will bring on sickness upon yourself. Many physical problems come directly from un-forgiveness. Some people feel that their pride was stumped upon. Many feel that they are in a position that no one can do me like this and get away with it. Remember what the bible says:

"Bless them that persecute you, bless, and curse not. Dearly beloved, avenge not yourselves, but rather give place unto wrath: for it is written, vengeance is mine; I will repay, saith the Lord." Romans 12:14,19

There will be hurt and pain in life, remember that God suffered pain and even was put in the hands of his enemies and died on the cross. God opened not his mouth, but bore persecution for the sake of our salvation, and remission of sins. He was the perfect blood sacrifice, so let's heed to God's call and be focused on him and his great love, and his acceptance of us. The bible says we are accepted into the beloved; we are the righteousness of God. Amen!!

Understanding is a tool that is helpful to all of us. If we use this tool as the scripture say, we will be happy. *"Wisdom is the principal thing; therefore get wisdom and with all thy getting get understanding" Proverbs 4:7.* The understanding of why people do certain things, helps us to deal with the problem, some how understanding lessens the pain, keeps you from taking it personal. The person that rejected you could have serious issues within themselves. One often acts out some behavior that began in their child hood. Some have a spirit of perversion, or a lust problem and some don't want responsibility of another.

7

Satan works on people's senses & weakness. He especially works on the eye gate. "*The lust of the eye, lust of the flesh and the pride of life, is all that is in the world*" I John. Often when some one is in inner pain and can't deal with life, and the struggles within, one will often find ways to medicate the pain within, most often, the first thing one will do is turn to a new relationship, or have an affair. "Thankfully, I did neither of them."

"God, in Jesus name, bless all those who are facing a broken relationship. Help them to feel your power right now. Give them a gracious and forgiving spirit towards anyone who has hurt them. Let their tomorrow be one that brings them joy, and inner peace and make them whole and shine your love in their soul. Let them feel your love, peace and mercy Bring restoration in their lives, replace what they have lost, bring them a true soul mate that will complement them and love them, and be faithful to them in Jesus name I pray." Amen!

Chapter Two
"Feeling Rejected"

Rejection in and of itself, can leave one feeling lonely, devastated, and unwanted. It brings on a feeling of inadequacy. Rejection hits each one in a personal way. It declares to you, that you're "not wanted" "see you later" "goodbye" "good written". That is why rejection can be tormenting to your mind, and cause severe low-self-esteem. I can't think of anyone who likes rejection in any way. We know some rejections are harder to deal with then others. In actuality, rejection comes in many ways, in whatever case, it is hurtful and painful. Some specific types of rejections hurt more than others.

Some grew up in homes where they were rejected; they grew up with the stigma of rejection, and than later, got into a relationship, only to be rejected again later in life. What pain and agony this could cause. Truthfully, everyone has been rejected in one way or another. Some people handle rejection different from others. Some have not taken it personally;

some learn to separate rejection from who they are. In other words, some have not given the rejecter power over them. Rejection, if not handled properly could and often times does, take you under, and leave you in severe depression, with no will power to move on.

The determined and goal oriented person, learns to separate the incident from who they are as a person. I have been rejected many times, but I learned to separate the rejection of others, and not take it personally, and declared who I am in Christ.

Surely rejection is not a welcome friend, and it does not feel good, but you learn to move on.

You tell yourself, that there is someone else in life that will be glad to have you be apart of their world. There are millions of people in the world, keep on moving forward. We are fearfully and wonderfully made.

God have accepted you and me, Hallelujah!!! We need to release this thought in our minds and speak with our mouths things that are positive, they that love to talk negative shall eat the fruit of what they say, so talk positive, tell yourself that you are accepted into the beloved, and are special to God, and that God did not make junk. You are so special to God, and to your loved ones. Sometimes those who are the closest to you separate themselves, because they can't deal with you in our state of rejection, they are waiting for you to get up and start all over, move on with life, and find strength and courage to fight.

When thoughts arise, and they will, we must reject them immediately; before those thoughts become strongholds in your minds. Strongholds can cripple you, and keep you from prospering. Your life becomes stagnant, and you end up stagnant, if you get stuck, and don't reject those constant thoughts of rejection. Satan brings us thoughts that are designed to destroy our will, your self-esteem and our zest and zeal to live. He wants to destroy us, and he uses our mind to battle with us. We can be healed, by making up in our minds to reject Satan and the thoughts of negativity He uses people to bring us down, he works twenty-four-seven, to find ways to tear up and destroy what God have made.

Ephesians 6:12

"For we wrestle not against flesh and blood, but against principalities, against powers, against rulers of darkness of this world, against spiritual wickedness in high places."

Healing will take place when we make up in our minds and declare that these rejections are not going to destroy me, and state several times a day, who you are in Christ. We have to tell the pain to move back, and get out of your way. Tell our thoughts to sit down and be under the subjection of God and his will. Let God heal you through prayer and fasting, and let God give you the desire to live on and enjoy life. Jesus can and will make you whole again, as he did for me. I was so entangled with my past life, and I did not know how I could go on in life without that relationship. I thought at times that life would be meaningless without him. Then Jesus stepped in and healed me, because I allowed him to heal me and restore and make me whole.

'Praise God" I learned to forgive and chose to let God help me understand this person's dilemmas, and for me not to

11

take it personally. No one is perfect, and neither was he. I did not want to be uncommitted, because of the imperfections of the marriage. Un-commitment starts with a thought. Thoughts become realities and bring on changes. People either recognize how important commitment is or they could care less about the word commitment. Some people's personal desires are more important to them than being committed. Commitment says "I am with you despite what else is out there that looks good or may feel good to me." It takes two people to be committed to each other to make a relationship work, and one person may be committed, but if the other is not, it will not work.

Some people medicate themselves through various means. Medicating helps some people cope with the lost but it doesn't heal you from the pain, it is just a temporary fix. For instance, pornography can control one's mind, and those images that one see through pornography, stay in ones mind and causes them to seek out what they have seen.

These images are implanted in the mind, and the person that watches pornography is moved with strong passions for these images. Unfortunately, pornography have led many to do some unseeingly things. The persons who are into pornographic scenes, often becomes target for Satan to use them in ways beyond their control. I have heard that many affairs have come to play and many other things such as: child molestation and many other forms of sexual crimes become prevalent in their lives.

Pornography brings on thoughts, and seeds become implanted in that person's mind and then seeds and thoughts become strongholds. This is when Satan uses your mind to cause you to do many bad things. You become trapped in your mind, you struggle with these thoughts and strongholds, until one day you take on affairs and this could lead you further and further into sin. You become a tool in Satan's hand. He begins to control you into deep, deep sins, and these sins destroy what they may have had before such as: their family, their salvation, and it become a cancer and destroy everything they ever had. Sin is not to be taken lightly. **There is a price to pay for your gratification**. There is too much at stake for you to put yourself in a position to lose out.

The spirit of perversion is raging greatly. The perverted spirit looks for ways to please their lust. I heard of a case where they even prey on young children, and molest these children, and have become serial child molesters. Many others look for ways to have kinky sex with those who model those whom they seen in pornography scenes or playboy books. These individuals are very unhappy, and are looking for ways to make them selves happy. When they finish one sex act, often they are still not satisfied, and began to look for more ways to please themselves.

They look for more intense sexual relationships to medicate the pain they are experiencing inside and to fill the voids or emptiness they are having.

If you can understand the satanic attack on people, you will be of an understanding heart, and not be angry and bitter against them, but you will actually feel sorry and sad for the person. This person needs severe pray, so we must not give into feelings of un-forgiveness and depression. We must not let Satan work on them and us too. Someone have to take a stand, so why can't it be you.

Understanding is priceless, and it will bring a resolve to any situation we face in life. This understanding will help anyone to take control of their minds, and thoughts, and cause one not to feel rejected, but understand the spirit powers of Satan, and what he uses to destroy people and their families. He will work with anyone who lets him. Male or female, it does not matter who it is, but he have an ulterior motive and that is to destroy us and our families. *"For Satan come to steal, to kill and to destroy."* He has made many tools available to people to destroy them. The computer sitting in your homes could be a tool for pornography and the chat room.

The book of James tells us that, *"we are drawn away by our own lust and are enticed." Lust brings sin, sin brings on death.* Realize the lust initially started with a thought in ones mind, whether the thoughts came by visual senses (the eye gate) or lustful feelings in the flesh, it must be dealt with. The penalty is too great for any one to play with fire. You will get burned. If thoughts that are detrimental are not dealt with and rejected immediately, strongholds are inevitable and then the acting out of these feelings is a sure thing.

Yes, "I was rejected" but, "yes, I was accepted into the beloved." Rejected by man, but accepted by God. Which is the best? The question I had to ask myself is, why make a God out of the pain of rejection? Unknowingly, I begin to make a god out of my pain and rejection. In reality, I began to idol my problems, by focusing on them so much. God was pushed further and further from my mind, because I was too engrossed with what had happened to me. I love God so much, and I have a close walk with God, but I did not respond properly to my rejection and I did not put the principles of the bible to work as I should have. I had to give account to God for my disobedience. By me leaving God out of things and trying to handle things my own way, I ended up even more devastated and depressed. It was not until I gave it over to Jesus and let him work it out and let him heal me and that is when I became whole.

I was pointing figures and sobbing over how I was left for someone else. I refused to be comforted by God, but fell into pity parties. I asked myself why would God allow this to happen? Before things got out of hand, with my marriage, I seen warning signs of things falling apart, but I did not think it would ever get to this. He was slipping away from me little by little. There was an all out attack on my marriage.

I made so many attempts for us to get help, but I was the only one that put effort in getting help. It takes two people to make a relationship work. Resistance after resistance was what I dealt with, until I woke up and smelt the coffee. I was not a bad person that some one would want to up and leave me, but on the other hand I was not perfect, and I had my flaws, but I loved and served God, and I loved my x-husband greatly. I am over that pain and rejection now, and I have no hard feelings toward him, but I now understand how one could come to the points of calling it quits.

The pressure of life with all of people's experiences make people sometime forget all about being committed. Thankfully, I am not bitter, but have moved on with my life, you can move on the same way.

God's grace and mercy brought me back to seeking him, and I sought God's forgiveness for my anger and bitterness, and un-forgiveness. Gratefully, my relationship with God grew more and more, as I allowed God to be God. Little did I know that God allows the cords of many relationships to be cut, so we must accept God's will. God surely have the power to revive and heal all relationships, but it's not his perfect will to mend every relationship, because some people are just not good for each other. Some people bring you down low, and that is all they do, is bring you down. Now I know that my marriage was one of the relationships that God did not revive. God have a divine plan and will for all of us, sometimes it might not be pleasing to us, but we must accept his will.

God restored me back to the place where I was before the breakup of my 30 plus year marriage. In fact, I have more zeal and zest for life now than before. I have a better appreciation for God now than ever before. He has filled the void that I experienced.

Psalms 51:12 *"Restore unto me the joy of thy salvation; and uphold me with thy free spirit". Psalms 51:1 say "Create in me a clean heart, O God and renew a right spirit within me. Cast me not away from thy presence and take not thy Holy Spirit from me."*

I used these words of King David, and applied it to my own life. I needed forgiveness for all the bitterness, resentment and un-forgiveness I had experienced from the break-up of my marriage. I needed God's help, after all, I began to run to and fro: from one city to another, seeking refuge and peace of mind, and I tried to find myself.

I stayed in the church, I continued going to church and praying and reading my bible, but I still needed healing and restoration.

God sent people around me to encourage me and pray with me. God sent angels to protect me and get me on my feet and survive. I had to push away pain and thoughts and the feelings of rejection. With all I went through, I can't find or think of anything that is better than serving God; despite who may leave you for someone else, regardless of how people reject you from their world, God said, I will never leave you or forsake you. *"God said, I will be with you until the end of the world."* God did not forsake me, but kept his loving arms around me. He would not let me go. He has restored me and made me whole again. **God will replace what you lost**. He will send someone who will be glad to have you; someone that will love all over you. Let God send you the right person. God wants to give you someone, but you must be whole for the new person. You must be whole in your mind, heart, thoughts, emotions, and mostly spiritually.

God is trying to send you someone special, but if you are stuck in the past, how can you go forward and love someone else, especially if you only think of who you lost?

It does take time to get over the person that you were in relationship with, but it will take much longer if we won't let go and let God. We can keep ourselves back by how we deal with the situation. We can ask God to help us to move on, and for God to break the soul-ties. Until the soul-ties have been broken, you can't go forward.

Philippians 3 says *"forgetting those things that are behind you and reaching forth unto those things which are before you. I press towards the mark for the prize of the high calling of God in Christ Jesus."*

If we become opened to newness, and not be stuck in the past, but are determined to move on with the present and are planning for the future, then great things will start to materialize. How can one receive a new relationship, while stuck in the old relationship? The bible uses a scenario as this, "how can you put new wine in an old bottle." Surrender right now your pain and grief to God. Come on, relax and let it go! Healing will begin and you will see and feel a difference in your life immediately, now you must resist the thoughts that will try to come back to you. Reject every negative thought, and send them back to the pits of hell. Walk in your God given authority. Your identity is not what happened to you, "but you are a chosen generation a royal priesthood", and you are not the victim; please throw away the victim mentality.

God will give you double for your trouble. I dare you to start praising and worshipping God, and get caught up into who God is to you, instead of what someone did to you. Praise your way out of your troubles. Acts 16 says, "Paul and

Silas prayed and praised God at midnight and their shackles were broken, and they were able to walk out of that prison." They did not let their problems get them down.

God wants us to love him, despite what is happening in our lives. God dwells in the midst of praise. Many battles in the bible were won, though praising God. God is all powerful and all knowing and can give victory in your every situation. All God have to do is speak to the situation as he spoke man and the world into existence.

Discover deep down who you are, drawing out the strength and courage that God gave you. Do something for yourself. Lose some weight, buy a new wardrobe, get involved and help others who are going through issues. Many times when you are alone, you will discover things about yourself.

I desired to lose weight for myself; I lost fifty pounds after my marriage broke-up. It was not from stress or depression, but God helped me with my will-power and I started eating healthy, and I feel so much better. For the first time in many years, I began to do things for me. I took some classes and I did settle down in another city, because for me, a new atmosphere made a difference in my healing process. God has worked wondrously in my life, and so will he work miracles in your life, if you let him. He will give you a new beginning, just ask him. My self-esteem has soared and I feel healthy and inspired to help others who are hurting, and have been rejected. That is why I wrote this book, so that others can do things much different than I did and heal quickly and smoothly.

It is time for you now. You have spent all of your energy on someone else, now pamper yourself. Go out sometimes and treat yourself to a new outfit, a nice dinner, and get your hair and nails done, take a vacation, and remember to help someone who is hurting. Give a kind word, encourage someone, pray with someone. Do shopping for someone, or run errands for them, you will discover a joy and peace in helping others. Don't dry up and die, but water life and live.

Chapter Three
"Surviving Divorce"

Through the years of raising a family of four daughters, I experienced many happy and joyful days. Time goes by so fast. I remember the joy of bringing them home from the hospital, and watching them grow up right before my eyes. The memories of what were and what is not now strikes me as, how so many changes could come overnight. The thirty plus years of marriage had several happy times and unforgettable memories of what a happy family should be like. So many Sundays we went to church and included God in our family's lives, and it was so hard to come to scrip with me being divorced and the reality of the whole thing. I must say that the initial shock of life alone was heart breaking; now I have grown to the idea and have moved on with my life, and still enjoying my relationship with God and my grown-up children.

I settled in Indianapolis, Indiana after the finality of my marriage. I was in Atlanta Georgia for a few months, but I did not find solace there, and I soon move here in Indiana and I must say, being here really helped me heal and move on with life. I really enjoy my new church home and family, and the new job that I have, they keep me so busy as well as being in the ministry. I did not have to be surrounded with so many memories of the past. It is truly a new beginning for me. That is not to say that memories don't come to my mind, because they do, but the memories are not painful as they once was, but are just thoughts of how God brought me out. Things that happened to me were just a part of my destiny.

Philip and myself raised four beautiful daughters, Camille, Kecia, Carla and April, and now have five grand sons and three granddaughters, so the thirty years brought fourth beautiful things that yet exist today, so all was not lost, they will always be my daughters and grand sons and grand daughters. "Praise God" All of my daughters were gone and grown up when this situation occurred, so for that I am so grateful.

I decided to look at the bright side of things, while divorce is something that no one really should take lightly, the reality of it is, sometimes it happens, and life must go on. "I chose to water life and live" and move forward. I am not stuck into what happened to me, I am not identified as a divorcee, but I am identified as a "Christian woman", who loves God. I am enjoying my relationship with God every day.

If I did not have God in my life at that time, no telling where I would be. Following the precepts of the bible, have guided and shed light in my life, and God has ordered my steps.

The beginning stages of being divorced I reacted much different than at the present. The reality of the end of an era of life with the person you loved, nearly took me for a loop. I was so in love with Phil. He was my high school sweetheart. We nearly did everything together, almost inseparable. I wondered how a close couple could as we were, quit. There were so many questions in my mind. I could hardly sleep, eat, and had little motivation to do any thing in the beginning. I cried day and night wishing things had not come to such an end. What was I going to do now was what I thought, and how can I carry on, and these questions haunted me for many months after the break-up. The break-up happened in the fall of 2002, and it now 2006, wow!

We tried to stay together, but things never worked out. Destiny had it to be this way. There was not enough room for any third parties in our relationship. It was a time where your heart dropped, and you felt as if you had hit rock bottom. You felt so low until you wonder if you could make it back up. I had wrapped my life and happiness in Phil. I wonder if I put him ahead of God. God wants to be first in our lives, and he will, if he has to, move the thing or person that you have put ahead of him out of the way.

I realized, I needed to prioritize my life. Between a husband and wife there is God, and he must not be left out, or you are sure to hit some bumps in the road. Don't get me wrong, God intends for couples to stay together and work very hard to make it work. It was in Genesis, where God said, "it is not good for man to be alone", and he brought Adam and Eve together, "and he told them to be fruitful and multiply". God definitely approves of family. The first commandment is for us to love the Lord God with all of our heart, mind and soul. The second commandment is that we love our neighbor as we love ourselves.

Months went by, and I was still trying to fill the tear in my heart. I did not hit the bottle or do drugs, but I sought comfort from people too strongly. Of course I prayed and asked people to pray for me. The pain did not seem to let up. I was so lonely, and felt so empty and unwanted. I thought over and over again that my love life would never be recaptured. After all, my ex-husband brought me a lot of years of happiness. He was my friend, lover and husband, confidant, and the father of my children.

All of a sudden, I was alone, my children were all grown and had their own lives to live, so I had just me to either do or die. Eventually, I fought to live and make things happen for myself. I became more compassionate to those people I knew who were divorced, or had broken relationships. Many times you don't know how people hurt, until you have been down that same road. When a person goes through divorce, they will see life in a whole new perspective. It can be an avenue of learning, growth and an awakening.

Time has been a healer for me. I now look back and see and remember all of the agony I went through, and I am so glad I didn't die in my pain. I am so thankful to God. You literally have to roll up your sleeves and fight hard to get through. You have to have faith to believe that you can conquer the devastation of divorce. Just like a surgical would have to heal, the wounds of divorce must heal through nurturing and time. The initial surgery brings on great pain, but each day you will feel better, if you do the proper things to promote healing. If you do certain things too fast after surgery, you slow down the healing process, and the wound could become infected; the same with divorce, you must find a healthy way to heal properly, so infection won't set up, and therefore be a delay in healing. Do you know that if a person is very low sick, but have a fight inside of them to live; they are more likely to overcome their illness than someone who has no fight in them. Fight to live, dare to overcome, look the obstacle in the face and say you will not destroy me. Be determined to conquer and survive or out live the detriment that passed your way. Persistence, Persistence, and more Persistence!

Chapter Four
"Grieving a Broken Relationship"

Grieving is a process that takes time to get through. There are so many normal stages of grief. Anger is one of the stages, as is denial. Even with so many stages of grief, we must allow God in, because grief can be deadly. It can take you down deep into depression. Depression will keep you in one stage of grief and will not allow you to heal.

Fighting grief is not good, but on the other hand grief should not linger and linger. God gives us his strength during our grief. His supernatural power will abide close by us. He is omnipotent (all-powerful) and he has all the power we need to get through any tragedy. Some people want to stay down in grief and depression. It is then that we reject the comfort, love and strength of the almighty God. God is a comforter and he comforts us in many ways. He often uses people to comfort us. If we let him handle it, our grief can be quickly gotten over, and if we allow the almighty to do things his way, he will surely bring healing.

There is a saying that "**time heals all wounds".** Whether it is one week, month or a year, it will surely come. Some heal quicker than others. Some are weaker than others, and some think differently about situations than others. We cannot try and compare the differences in time that people are healed, because for many people, they do things to keep their minds off of things, while others want to ponder, think and grieve.

We as individuals look and feel things differently. One may look at the death of a loved one with a positive mind, knowing that their loved one is not suffering, and that they are in a better place, and another person, might look at death in a more sorrowful way; They may feel like they can't make it without that person, or they may be in denial and angry.

It's that same way with a divorce or a broken relationship. You can choose to look at the bright side of things, or get drowned in all of the negative things of divorce. Our personality plays a part in it. We are either a pessimist or an optimist, but if we trust in God and not who or what we are, than things will be different and positive for us, because once we are saved; we are supposed to take on the mind of Christ.

There is nothing wrong with grief. It is healthy to grieve, and because each of us grieves differently, no one should put a time limit on another's grief process. Individuals, sometimes do things different from other individuals, so we should not beat up some one that grieves differently than you would.

What part does God have when we are grieving? God changes the scope of our grief process through his divine power and strength. While we are weak and handle things in a human way, God comes along and changes things, by giving us his strength, his courage, and comfort, and he gives us the proper way of dealing with our complexities in life as grieving.

The apostle Paul said it like this, "We don't grieve as others that have no hope." That is a powerful statement. This is true, but even in the bible, there were a mourning period for someone that died, so there is an expectation for us to take time and grieve. We can use that statement and apply it to anything that we will face in life. For we know that God is a "rock of Offense" as well as a "comforter" "a lifter up our heads." You may be bowed over in grief, but soon you will be lifted up, some sooner than others. The more we yield to God's comfort and healing, the quicker we will be healed. God deals with each of us on our own level. It is God's desire that we come up to the level that he will give you swift healing. God is a gentleman, and he is touched with the feelings of yours and my infirmities. Even Jesus wept when Lazarus died. In life we must say, if this happened to me, then there will be some good that will come from it.

Jesus loves us so much, and we were made in his image. He took special knowledge of his creation, in particular, when he made mankind. He said, "He would never leave us nor forsake, us, and that he would be with us unto the end of the world." God care for us, the scripture say, "cast all of your cares on him for he cares for you and it say to come boldly to the throne of grace, that we may obtain help in the time of need."

There is no greater love any where beside God. It is God's love that we can lean and depend on in our times of grief. He will take the hurt away, and mend the broken pieces of your heart together. God understand the grief that we suffer when we lose someone that is near and dear to our hearts, and he understands the stages of this type of grief, but remember God' grace and tenderness can make the process go so much more smoothly if we allow his powerful love to embrace and strengthen our hearts.

Joyce Meyer said, "Jesus can heal you everywhere you hurt." I like that because he is the only one I know that can heal you everywhere you hurt, because he really is the only one who knows everywhere we hurt.

Chapter Five
"Being Single Again"

Singleness in today's society can be very challenging. You almost have to learn all over again how to be single effectively. If you have been married for a while, and become single again, it can be very challenging, particularly if you leave home from your parents and get married and then are thrust back into being single. If this is the case, it is hard because you have virtually always lived with someone, but now it is just you and only you, as far as in the physical.

When two people are married, they become one half of the whole and the spouse is the other half of the whole. When you are single, there is no more two halves, but there is one whole person, Of course in the eyes of God he sees a couple as one.

When you are single, there is a big difference in your life. It then becomes you and God alone in a spiritual way. You learn how to be whole in your ways, thoughts and habits. There is no one but you to do everything that needs to be done. Taking out the garbage, doing the dishes, cleaning and making the entire ends meet financially. This takes some getting use to, especially if you shared another income and resources of your spouse.

On a positive note, when you are single, you have the leisure to not cook or clean on days that you don't want to. There are advantages and disadvantages in being single. Some personalities do very well being single, while other personalities struggle being single. Which ever the case, we must learn to be whole and single rather than single and not whole. Whole means being totally one in whom you are. There must be wholeness in your mind, body and spirit.

If you have a whole pie, nothing has been cut, or removed but is perfect in its entirety. The pie acts alone, it doesn't need a slice added to it, neither does it need any ingredients added to it, because it is complete all by itself. That's the way we must be, before we can be united with someone else in marriage. When someone marries, we come to the marriage table well in our mind, body and spirit, a wholesome person.

True, singleness may bring loneliness, but with me, I experienced loneliness, but it does not take away my being whole. I am complete in Christ, that is my wholeness, yet I desire companionship. You must know who you are in Christ first. I personally would rather be with someone than to be alone. That is just me, but others may feel they do not want to have the possibility of another let down. Real wholeness comes through knowing Christ. It is God's spirit on the inside of you that completes us. The scripture says, "We are complete in him." "Praise God, I am complete, you are complete in God! Hallelujah!!

When a marriage occurs, two complete or entire people come together, and there is yet greater strength there, because both of them are complete. The grief period should be over when you enter into another relationship, so that you will not bring sickness into the new relationship.

Just as we are praying for a good mate, so is the other person praying for a good, well, wholesome, anointed mate. That is why there needs to be some time to get over the person that left you. They need to be out of your system, and so you can properly receive the new person that God wants to give you.

For some it does not take long to get over some one and for others, it takes a long time. Some time putting distance between you and person that you had a relationship with will help you quickly come back to being yourself again.

Apostle Paul said in I Corinthians 7, "*It is good if you can abide alone as he is*" He knew that your availability for God's work increases when you are single. You have time to glorify God, and pray as long as you want to. The single person according to the Apostle Paul "care for the things of the Lord, how they may please God, both in body and spirit, while the married person careth for the things of the world, how they may please their mate."

You can choose what you will do as the Lord pleases. As a single person, you can fast without having to get permission or make sure that it is suitable for the two of you. There is a lot of freedom in being single. Some are gifted in this area of being single. Some get involved, so they are seldom lonely, while others are more laid back, and are not so out going, and struggle with maintaining a life to include others.

There are marriages that each spouse lives very independent of the other, and there are other marriages where the couple does almost everything together. It is easier maintaining singleness if you had a virtually independence in your marriage, the couples that were inseparable find it much more difficult being single again.

My marriage was very close knit and we did almost everything together, so I feel it was harder for me trying to be single again, but I am over that now. God has taught me how to depend upon him. Sometimes, we can depend too much on the other person and don't leave room for God to do nothing.

God is a jealous God; he will not have anyone over him in our lives. He wants to be number one in our lives. Often times, we put our mates as number one without realizing it. That spouse can become an idol before the face of God, and God will surely tear down any idols in our lives. We must be so careful, not to offend God and have the sin of idolatry.

Could God be doing surgery on us? Refining and reshaping us for him and his kingdom, instead of our own kingdom. Maybe some of us got lost in the sauce of marriage. We belong to God, and we have to remember that and to put God first in everything we do, or we have to pay the consequences.

God want us to have a loving and healthy marriage, but God never intended for a marriage to be your main satisfying portion. Only God can be God in your life. Can't anybody do you like Jesus?

God decided for me to be single right now for many reasons. You must ask God if this is the case with you, but I know God had to get my attention. Phil was my whole world, everything centered around him. It was my aim and goal to please him very highly. Was God jealous of my too strong of devotion towards him? I see now that many times unconsciously I put him before God. You see, you can over do anything. The scripture say, "Be temperate in everything."

God often times allows the person you put above him to reject you, to get your focus right. Matthew says, "Seek ye first the kingdom of God and his righteousness and all these things will be added unto you." Keeping things in their proper perspective will keep things flowing smoothly in our lives. During this time of your being single, hopefully will be a time of examining ourselves and perfecting the flaws in our lives.

It's a time for living holy before God. It's also a time for building up us and making our relationship with God right. It's a good time to do some soul searching, and pay close attention to the things of God concerning where we really are in our relationship with God.

We should live as though we are married to God. This is a good time to shape and develop a close and intimate relationship with God. Being single, allows you to have quality time to build strong bonds with God, and to find more and more ways to please him. Worshipping God builds strong bonds and cords that can't be easily broken. Take advantage of your singleness, until God sends you someone special to marry.

There is often a void in your life after a broken relationship; however, God can fill that void with his spirit. He can fill that feeling of loneliness. Staying in his word, will give you a satisfied feeling and make that empty feeling vanish. The more you pray, worship and praise him, the more you will begin to feel whole and fulfilled. His word is alive and can make alive every dead area in our lives. If your spirit is broken, his word is a repairer and healer. He will make the crooked places straight, and bring down mountains that have set up in our minds. His word is like a hammer, which will hammer out every imperfection we may have.

It is all in the word. Can't no one fulfill like God. Whatever you need him to be, it is in the word. Work the word, and be fulfilled. Tear down strong holds by using God's word. Every obstacle must flee through God's word, his word is like fire, it will burn out every feeling of hate and revenge and it will burn up every feeling of low self-esteem. For if you have Jesus, you have got it going on! If you are accepted into the beloved, it does not matter if someone rejects you, when God have accepted you.

If God be for you, who on earth can be against you. We don't have to fight our own battles, and I am glad about it, so rest your minds.

LORD I THANK YOU

GOD I THANK YOU FOR THIS TIME OF BEING SINGLE. YOU GAVE ME A CHANCE TO GET MY PERSPECTIVE TOGETHER, AND YOU GOT MY ATTENTION BACK TOTALLY ON YOU, AND FOR THIS "I THANK YOU" YOU HEALED ME FROM A BROKEN HEART, AND FOR THIS, "I THANK YOU" YOU MADE ME WHOLE AGAIN, AND FOR THIS, "I THANK YOU" LORD YOU KEPT MY MIND STAYED ON YOU AND FOR THIS, "I THANK YOU" LORD OUR RELATIONSHIP HAVE GROWN VERY CLOSE, AND LORD, FOR THIS, "I THANK YOU" LORD, YOU HELPED ME FORGIVE HIM, AND LORD FOR THIS, "I THANK YOU" LORD, GOD, YOU EVEN TOOK THE HURT AND PAIN AWAY, AND FOR THIS, "I THANK YOU" LORD, YOU SHOWED ME HOW TO BE SINGLE AGAIN, AND FOR THIS "I THANK YOU" LORD, FOR ALL YOUR GOODNESS, "I THANK YOU ONCE, NO I THANK TWICE, BECAUSE YOU PAID THE PRICE!!!

Chapter Six
"A Bright Tomorrow"

Hope is what we look to when we have reached a detour in our lives. Without hope, dreams, visions, aspirations, ambitions and future planning would be insignificant. With hope in our heart and mind, there are reasons to believe for changes. Yesterday may have brought devastation or broken promises, but if there is an array of hope, one will feel some spirit of possibilities.

Tomorrow should be intertwined with the word hope. We can say, there is a tomorrow to make your dreams come true. Tomorrow holds for all of us promises. You can dust yourself off and start a brand new day of Grace. With each day that God gives us, we can shape a day positive or negative; it's up to us what we do in a given day.

Whether the sun is out or it's pouring down raining or a there is a snowing blizzard, we can be happy and hope for a better weather day tomorrow or the next day. Believe it or not, we can make things happen, or we can let them die.

Why not make each day count towards a positive goal. One thing to start with in each day is a beautiful attitude. Our attitude will determine the outcome of any day. Regardless what we may face, we can set the tone of any given day by our attitude. In reality, your body does not always feel good when you wake up. The thing we should ask our selves each day is, will this pain in my body or situation I'm facing determine or control my brand new day that God gave us, or will we stay in control of these things by having a good attitude and ponder what good this day may bring.

God said in his word, "Occupy until he comes back." There is the commandment from God, who makes each day. If you must be bed ridden because of illness, one can still look at the bright side of that; we can be thankful that we have a bed to rest in, and be thankful that you can rest, maybe there will be more time for you to read the bible, and more time to pray and just take a breather from it all. Looking on the positive side of things we face every day will light up your spirit, and will prompt you to fight for the victory of that day.

It is no wonder why the bible say "this is the day that the Lord has made, we shall rejoice and be glad in it." That is such a powerful statement, because it signals that the Lord made this day and because he made it, good can come out of each day. God said to rejoice with each day made. He did not say, if things are going well to rejoice, but to rejoice with each day, no matter what's happening.

The prefix "re" means repeat again or bring back. Come back to joy, bring back joy. Rejoice because we have a whole new day to be productive, work, pray, eat, shop, live, sleep, read, learn. Worship and praise God, love someone, encourage others, visit the sick, and embrace our loved ones and the list goes on and on.

Many ask God to order their steps with each new day. What a wonderful way to begin a day. Asking for God's guidance, will surely make a huge difference with what and how we face that day. You will be surprised at how your prayer will make each day an awesome experience. He will lead and guide us around things that could be detrimental; He could spare car accidents and many mishaps and confrontations that would have occurred. Praise our God and King!

What can I do tomorrow that I didn't get to do today or yesterday, or even last week or last year? It's a brand new beginning. A time to not only reflect on many possibilities, but also a time to correct or change things that we did or did not do in the past. We certainly can learn many things from the past that will help us in our decisions for tomorrow.

Maybe, we could go on and enroll in that class or major it's not too late to go to school or take a class to get your G.E.D. This would be one of the many things you could concentrate on for tomorrow. What about shedding a few pounds and taking time to exercise for health reasons or just to improve your looks.

Many of us have dreams and aspirations that are just lying dormant. Well on tomorrow these dreams could awaken, and you will be on an upward journey for you and countless others. Thinking of tomorrow should bring us an array of hope to accomplish your dreams and visions.

Your tomorrow will be what you make it to be. One thing for sure, it does not have to be a repeat of yesterday, and for some, we need to repeat some of the good things that we did. Learning to listen to God for direction and guidance should be at the top of the list. We could avoid so many pitfalls, if we look to God for his divine will in our lives.

Proverbs 3 say *"In all your ways acknowledge him, and he will direct your paths." Ps 119 says "the steps of a good man are ordered by God, Thy word is a lamp unto my feet and a light unto my path."*

In humble gratitude of each new day, and for the school of experience, we could certainly put forth effort to succeed and do better. There is always room for improvement. Doing a good job yesterday only means tomorrow we can do great. God wants us to learn from our past mistakes or past failures and turn them into tomorrow's victories. The lessons of our yesterday should bring us to gainful rewards. Realizing that it is in him (Jesus) that we move, live and have our being, so through God all things are possible to him that believe. God will not put on us no more than we can bear.

Plan tomorrow by faith. Take your faith out on the limb, and believe God for the impossible. For without faith, it is impossible for us to please God. So many things I can think of that I received from God by going out on the limb in belief. The same can be accomplished with you through your faith. Release your faith and receive your miracles, blessings, and answered petitions.

Get up from being stuck in yesterday and awaken your horizons with each new passing day. Arise and blossom, it's inside of you; pulling it out of you in belief, you have nothing to lose. All things are possible to him that believeth. We stand firm on that scripture when we face our tomorrows. If you refuse to believe in yourself, well start out by believing in God. God's supernatural power can transform all of our problems into triumphs. He is the lifter up of our heads. He is our battleaxe, our comforter, our hope for tomorrow, our joy in sorrow, our rose of Sharon, the everlasting father and the prince of peace.

Let God's warm array of love bring you back from yesterday's defeats. God's love will overshadow any tragedy or faulty encounters we have had. You can come back from whatever troubles you had to deal with in the past. Scarlet O'Hara, that played in the movie "Gone with the wind", said that "there is hope of tomorrow" What power those words declare, because that statement declares, no matter what your past was, it can all be changed in your tomorrow.

Where would we be without hope? If we had nothing to hope for, we all would walk and live in defeat. There would be nothing to look forward to, nothing to plan for, and nothing to dream of. Thank God we do have hope, and it's because of Jesus, We have hope of eternal life in heaven. We have the hope that bad things will change into good things.

Bad marriages and relationships can be changed, Because of our hope of a better tomorrow. Hope and tomorrow goes hand in hand, because both of the words signify an event of the future. Both are inspiring to the believer and especially to those who have had to deal with problem after problem, defeat after defeat.

Those who invest in stocks and bonds realize that their rewards will come in their tomorrow. Same as a freshman in high school or college, they realize that graduation will happen sometime in their future, but they have hope for a victorious experience. They are hoping for their tomorrow, they will see what they have worked so hard to obtain. As a freshman you can't see in the physical, your graduation and degree, but nothing can strip them of the hope of it.

That's the beauty of tomorrow. We hope for what tomorrow can bring. Those who have experienced broken relationships, divorce, death of a significant other or life's obstacles can take comfort and have hope in their tomorrow. So many breath taking events, which can brighten up any one's day is awesome. Let's reach out in hopes of a wonderful tomorrow and a bright future that God want to give all of us.

"Tomorrow, the Sun will come out"

Oh tomorrow, you will bring sunshine for this so many of us will truly be kind. We are waiting, waiting and waiting for you tomorrow. When you come, it gives us hope and melts away our sorrow. We are hoping that you, tomorrow will bring a day, that we won't need to borrow. We want to feel the shining sun, so that all of us can have a day of fun. What joy you bring to so many faces. You know, you can take us so many places. Thank you tomorrow, for giving us hope deep down inside, we know life is no joke. Tomorrow is so wonderful and real. We can't fake it, but we have to make it, that's the deal. Please hurry tomorrow, with all that you hold, you know to us, in our hands, tomorrow can turn to gold. Sun, please hasten your arrival, so we can take part. Don't delay, because it will only break my heart. Good, and loving tomorrow, we gladly look forward to you. Day after day, after day, to fight back being blue we love you tomorrow!!!

Chapter Seven
"Fighting Your Way Back to Happiness"

To boldly attack anything that causes pain is one way to fight forcefully. Going after something forcefully is what you must do to get back your happiness. Things in life have a way of somehow stripping you of the happiness that we have spent hours and years building; it takes a lot of time to get a relationship where it should be, but it could be torn up overnight.

If you want something bad enough, you will do whatever it takes to get that. So long as it doesn't involve hurting or tearing down someone else. Happiness is something that is very valuable to all of us. You can find happiness in "contentment". The bible clearly tells us "to be content in whatever state we are in", which means we can be happy in whatever circumstance we may find ourselves in.

There could be chaos all around, but on the inside of us we can be happy. Happiness is a state of mind. There is so much to be thankful for, and if we spend time thinking of how blessed we are, we should be happy. If you were unfortunate to have had a broken relationship, surely this will bring some unhappiness.

Everyone wants to live a life of happiness. Happiness for one may involve one thing, while for another, it is totally different. Regardless of how each of us define happiness, it is safe to say, that it means a great deal to us. Happiness is something that brings joy, peace of mind, a state of satisfaction.

With all of the attributes of happiness one would find it worth while to fight for happiness, after all it has so much to offer.

We seek happiness in many ways every day, unlike sadness, we do not seek to be unhappy, but sometimes it finds us. The benefits of being happy is worthy of us fighting for it. We want happy marriages, relationships, childhood, family life, and the list goes on and on. People spend hundreds and thousands of dollars trying to be happy, the state of being happy is worth more than a thousand words.

When we encounter anything that threatens our happiness, we put up defenses and we put up a fight to keep things as they are, because our happiness means so very much to us. We have found ways to build up to happiness in our lives, so, we most likely are not going to lie down and lay dead, when it is threatened. When we have had to deal with divorce or a broken relationship, we sometimes find ourselves wondering, is it worth fighting for happiness again, after experiencing such trauma. We have to take it by force. Our happiness means too much to us. We can't sit down and give up, because something in our lives was overturned.

Unhappiness many times leads to depression and hopelessness. On the other hand, unhappiness will make some people put up a fierce fight to get their happiness back. Some have determined in their minds that they are not going to quit, but fight, because happiness is a good feeling, it brings us too much, to just throw it away.

True happiness comes from knowing God, and when you know God, and are in relationship with him, this experience will cause you to reach heights of happiness unknown to many. It is no wonder the bible say, rejoice in the Lord, and again, I say rejoice. Your joy and happiness is very important to your walk with God. God makes the husband and wife's relationship to flourish with untold joy. The joy of the Lord is our strength, so it's important to have a true bonding relationship with the Lord.

Can't nobody, anywhere make you happy, like Jesus, and there is no friend that will stick closer to you than Jesus. It is so important to know where happiness really comes from, and how it is maintained and fulfilled by your relationship with God. When you have God, all of the other relationships are so much smoother and happier. People do a lot to bring joy and happiness to their lives, but Jesus can bring joy and happiness in its totality.

When you know Jesus, you will be so happy, because you know someone who is all powerful, all knowing and present everywhere. It's important to know what you are truly longing for. Things on this earth will not fulfill the deep hunger of wanting to know and be in fellowship and relationship with God. Our soul on the inside needs a supernatural God in our lives, and God is there for you, in fact he is waiting to be in relationship with you.

Jesus says in Matthew, "Come unto me all ye who are laden and burdened, take my yoke upon you, and learn of me, for my yoke is easy and burden is light, and ye shall find rest for your souls." Some of us need to strive to know God and to receive the infilling of the Holy Spirit, and watch things change for you completely. This is a guarantee.

I did not find true happiness until I gave my life to God. I realize that the fulfillment and real happiness in life came from being a born again believer. Meaning, being baptized in Jesus name and receiving the Holy spirit, and when you receive the Holy spirit, you will begin to speak in another tongue or language. That is the evidence that you have been filled with God's spirit. It is so very real, and it is the best feeling ever!

When I was married, I experienced great happiness with Phil, but it is no comparison to the real happiness and peace of mind that comes from knowing God, in the pardon and separation of my sins. I had the Acts 2:38 experience, where Peter spoke and preached repentance of sins, and being baptized with water, and receiving the gift of the Holy Ghost.

Thank God for his love and devotion of us, so much so, that he sent his only begotten son in the earth to die on the cross for our sins, that we may have hope of eternal life with him in heaven. What a blessing to know this God I serve, which satisfies you inside and out. What a love relationship. If you really want true happiness, seek God.

You hear of people doing things as eating, having sex, doing drugs and alcohol, going shopping and traveling etc. to make them happy. These are unhealthy channels to find happiness. True, we need to do some of the things mentioned such as traveling and shopping, but it should not be a tool to find happiness. You should already have happiness when you go on vacation or shopping.

Psychological happiness is only a temporary fix to real happiness. You will need to keep repeating these same things over and over again. Fighting for happiness should be done in perspective. There are natural things that brings happiness but also there are spiritual things that bring real happiness that last. God's spirit works on our natural man and the psychic. His love and power goes way beneath the surface of our hearts and make the needed corrections, which will inevitably bring happiness.

Children find happiness in going to amusement parks, where many adults find happiness in dating and getting married. We spend big money on making our dates happy, and even more money on our weddings and honey moons. Naturally, if the relationship crumbles, we tend to breakdown, fall apart, and reach for something that will cause us to feel happy in order to fill the void.

When someone or something tries to destroy the well being of your happiness, we immediately put up defenses, and seek to wart off. That's our natural mechanisms to fight for what is yours and what we have spent years building. There is also a group of people who don't fight back, they give up real soon, they feel as if there's no hope, they throw in the towel, go into depression, they give up on what they have invested so much time and energy on.

The bible tells us to contend for the faith. Contend is another word for fight. Also, in our natural lives we must contend for what belongs to us. Not give in, because we see something going sour. Our heavenly father has the power to mend broken places in our lives. He is able, and he is willing to help us, but we have to do something. We know that if we do certain things or get involved with something or someone, that there is a possibility that this will be bad for the welfare of your life, relationship, marriage, job, kids, and finances so we could fight before something happens.

We have all heard of preventive maintenance. This is fighting for a cause before something happens. We have to watch and pray, because your adversary walks about as a roaring lion, seeking whom he may devour.

He absolutely hates couples and families, and he wants to tear them up, but we can many times step in and stop him. Other times, when we have put up a fight to save our homes and relationships, nothing seem to change, but at least, if it goes down, it will go down with a fight.

It takes two to make a marriage, relationship work. If one of the partners refuse to fight with you, and is set to leave or be with someone else, the book of I Corinthians 7, say "a person is not under bondage in that case, and that if a person wants to leave, let him or her leave."

49

In that case, you can definitely fight for a healthy mind, body and spirit. Start over, and move on to better things. Fight depression, defeat, and being the victim. Instead of settling to be the victim, settle for being the victor. Be a Victor and triumphant with your God and your new life. Something good is going to come out of your lost.

Let's lift up our heads and fight to keep our relationship with God strong and to not let life's blows take us under. God knows how to revive and restore. He is going to give you back, what was stolen from you. *Jeremiah 29:11 say, "for I know the plans I have for you, plans to prosper you and to give you an expected end."*

Putting your trust in God will keep your spirits lifted, and it will give you a determination to get your joy back. Fight with force and with the word of God. Let the word of God work for you in all that you may be facing. Allow God to bathe you in his strength. He will carry you when you are too weak to face some challenges. His aim and goal is to give you the desires again to push forward in life and happiness. He is utmost concerned about your relationship with him, he want to be close to you, and walk and talk with you, and give you the real happiness that you deserve.

Chapter Eight
"Surviving Loneliness"

Loneliness is a strong feeling of being alone or in the state of mind that you are all alone. It could be a feeling of emptiness or extreme void of purpose or desire. It has been known for some devastating results. It is a feeling that makes one to feel unneeded, or there is no purpose for you being into existence, you feel not useful in anything, it's just a feeling that one is facing his world all alone, and that you do not belong.

Loneliness can and will cause your heart to ache. It also have caused some people to even leave this world, because they could not deal with the pain of being alone and felt useless and hopeless. Loneliness has a way a working on your self-esteem. Everyone does not feel this as a result of a broken relationship. Some people know how to stay busy and are focused on other things, while others are more outgoing than others and can get around friends and family, and become involved with them.

When some people find themselves feeling lonely, many of them become swamped with engagements, appointments, meetings, and so on, and this keeps their mind and life busy; therefore alleviating the feeling of lonely.

There are many people who are lonely and married at the same time, so you can be married and in relationship, but yet be lonely, because of different circumstances. Some couples spend little to no time together, and some spend ample time together and are still lonely, because their needs while together are not met. One can be in a crowd of people and yet feel that they are alone and empty.

People wants to feel a sense of acceptance and the satisfaction of belonging to someone or to something, and when that need is not met, they still find them selves feeling so lonely. Many are vulnerable to these needs, if they are not met. Love is something that every one need. There is within us all, a need to receive love and a need to give love.

Love is what makes a well rounded person feel secure and happy in themselves. A person that loves you could be thousands of miles away, but if you know that this person(s) love you, it satisfies a strong need. Having a loving and supportive person in your life can ease and prevent the feelings of loneliness that can creep up on you and therefore having an impact on you both emotionally and physically.

A little initiation on ones part to get involved in groups or social events, and finding friends, or start volunteering and especially getting in a good church home and become active, will bring on true motivation and little by little those feelings of loneliness, isolation and not feeling needed or purposeful will start to disappear. Your motivation to live and fight will return when you start making some effort to get out of the rut of the deadly disease of loneliness. You have to push yourself to get involved, and get out and help others, and speak positive concerning yourself and whatever circumstance you find yourself in. There is someone waiting to be your friend. There is someone that needs you. You are that special person that could make some others smile and laugh and feel worth living. There is greatness in all of us. No one is perfect, but everyone has some good in them.

Find ways to bring out that goodness and be sure and share your goodness, because someone right next door could need someone to show them love and care. We all need a loving smile, a warm embrace, a kind word. Will you be the first to give this to those that need it?

Deep down in the heart, there is a longing for fulfillment, and one of the needs of a human is the need to be with others, if only in spirit. We have a need to share our lives with someone. To have someone to share your heart with, even your ups and downs will make life easier. People want someone to eat with, shop with, spend days together, and just to be a part of someone's life.

The bible say in the book of Genesis, "it is not good for man to be alone", so no wonder there is a need to be included in something and with someone. Staying busy will work wonders in easing and preventing the feeling of loneliness. We should realize that there are many other people who feel the same way you feel, and who would love to have you as a part of their lives. Reach out and touch someone today.

Most people don't show loneliness, but deep down inside, it is there. The ache of loneliness rest deep down beneath the surface, in fact many do not realize that they are lonely. God made us not to be alone, but to be together.

There is a saying, which is true: "Together we stand, divided we fall" how true a statement, because when a group of people come together and are united, great things come to pass and nothing can defeat a group of united bodies.

I must admit that loneliness was the one of the biggest hurdles for me to overcome, because I was married for over thirty years, and in a close and loving relationship. I have not had to live alone, and it takes some getting use to. Sure there are advantages of living alone, but for me, I enjoy living in a family setting. It is hard to break the cycle of being with someone, and especially, if you were close, and inseparable, but God gives grace and he takes this time for you and him to get closer and more intimate than ever. I really fought being alone, and felt severely lonely in the beginning of the separation.

With time I am doing better, but I still at times feel alone, but now instead of the feeling overtaking or controlling me, I do something about it, and become engrossed with many other things, which keeps me busy. I found that reaching out to others who are really hurting helps me in my needs of healing. Spreading comfort and good cheer to others who are in need has a two-fold-blessing. You are helping to lift up others while helping your self get out of the slump of loneliness and depression.

When the spirit of complaining tries to raise its ugly head, God shows me someone who is in much worst shape than I am in. There is so much to be thankful for. There are so many people that are incarcerated, in mental hospitals, and nursing homes and without day-to-day needs, so we have so much to give God praise for. "What a friend we have in Jesus" He will heal every longing and aching need, who best can help us, but Jesus Christ. He will fill the deepest voids in our life. He knows how to turn the rain to sunshine, and give you a brand new reason to live and let live. It is God who is our satisfying portion. We need him in our daily walk. He is the ultimate way out of our any emotional or physical prison. He is the lifter up of our heads. The joy of the Lord is our strength. That is the perfect answer to loneliness.

God cares about your feelings and concerns. He is touched with our weaknesses and pain, and feelings of loneliness, insecurity, low self-esteem, rejection, hurt and broken heart, but there's good news my friend, God is a repairer and restorer of the breech. He will mend your broken heart and give you new people that will be glad to love and receive you. Listen, God knows best concerning all of us. Where we try to fix it, God has made the diagnosis and is prepared to do surgery on our heart aches.

Release it all to God, for he is the only one who truly understands you and what you are feeling, experiencing and he knows how to fix the problem. He will comfort you at your lowest point in life. I can attest to that, because I felt as if I was no longer needed or wanted, but Jesus stepped in put his loving arms around me and encouraged me to get up and push and praise him. He actually many times put the spirit of praise on me, which entail strengthened me and brought new hope, joy, and the desire to live again. I did not know what to do after such a lost, but Jesus stopped by and picked me up, he gave me incentive and the will to make it, and to live and to continue my walk with him. That is why I can say now, that I am still standing, I am still alive, *"No weapon formed against me shall prosper, and every tongue that shall rise against me in judgment, I will be able to condemn"* Isaiah 54:17

As the Lord taught me and is teaching me is to praise him and worship him in the midst of calamity. There are answers to prayer just through praise and worship. There is healing in praising him.

There is sure victory in worshipping God. That was mine and your answer to these situations that we are facing. Even when you don't feel like praising him, that is when to start praising him, because you will confuse the enemy, and the victory will be won and you will soon overcome by the blood of the lamb and the word of your testimony, so speak it out, say it, the victory is mine.

Soon the memory of who rejected you will have little significance to you. You will not have hard and unforgiving feelings toward that person when you get wrapped up and tied up in Jesus. You will have a new focus. God does things in his time, he is allowing you through time and space to heal from the brokenness, but you will come out of this situation much stronger than you could ever imagine. God will give you double for your trouble, and your later will be greater than your past. You will experience and have so much more after the storm than you ever had before. You thought you were happy before, but wait and see what happiness God has in store for you.

I have a common friendship with my x-husband, and that is all. I rarely, if ever talk with him, but we are at peace with one another, as God would have it. God will give you the grace to love the person in a Godly way. I am receptive to the new love God is going to send me. Psalms 23 is a reality when it says, "The Lord restored my soul."

The more you stay in the bible, the less lonely you will feel, because the promises of God are yea and amen. The word of God won't lie to you.

There are so many promise scriptures and verses in the word that is filled with hope. Let the rich word of God ease your loneliness and hurt, let his word fill your heart with real joy.

Jesus is a rock in our weary land. In fact he is a rock of offence, our bridge over troubled water, when feeling lonely. God wants us to have more of him and all these things in life will be added to us. There is room for all of us to get closer to God, and let his Holy spirit rule our spirit, let his spirit allow us to love and forgive and be happy again. I am a witness that he will do it.

All through the night, I felt God's loving arms all around me. He is right there with me and you. He cares about all of our needs; he often rocks me to sleep. He holds my head in his lap, and often carries me into spiritual places that only he can take me to. He is a one of a kind lover and companion. I can tell him things that I can't share with anyone else. God's strong love for me satisfies and sustains me. I love him and he loves me.

Isaiah 54:5-8 *"For thy maker is thine husband; the Lord of hosts is his name, and they redeemer the Holy one of Israel; the God of the whole earth shall be called. For the Lord hath called thee as a woman forsaken and grieved in spirit, and a wife of youth when thou wast refused, saith thy God. For a small moment have I forsaken thee, but with great mercies will I gather thee. In a little wrath I hid my face from thee for a moment; but with everlasting kindness will I have mercy on thee saith the Lord thy* Redeemer.

Chapter Nine
"Pray & Praise Your
Way Out of Distress"

Acts 16:25 describes the effectiveness of payer and praise. *"And at midnight Paul and Silas prayed, and sang praises unto God: and the prisoners heard them and suddenly there was a great earthquake, so that the foundations of the prison were shaken; and immediately all the doors were opened, and everyone's bands were loosed."* What an example in this writing. There are many, many books and writings in our world, but there is a living book which has life in it. There are so many examples of how we should live our daily lives, as well as how we should respond to trials and pressures of life. No one is exempt from problems and hard times.

There were many hard things experienced by the early church and we can learn from the examples written in the bible. Prayer, Praise and Worship and fasting were some of the main tools used to abort the snares and traps that crossed their paths. We have to learn to deal with difficulties in the spirit realm. For the weapons of our warfare are mighty through God to the pulling down of strong holds. The battle is often in our minds and many of our thoughts can either make us or break us. Thoughts could become strongholds. These thoughts come to hold you captive or imprison you. Our thoughts could lead us in a path of destructions. We often become a prisoner of our own minds. We are what we think. We have to dismiss negative thoughts immediately so the thoughts won't take root and grow. When roots grow they become hard to root up.

Take charge of our thoughts through the word of God. Reject bad and unhealthy things that so easily come to your mind. Our enemy, which is Satan, uses our mind as his number one battleground against us. He takes life's circumstances and pounds them in our minds, in order to destroy your energy, self-esteem, health, mind and most of all a healthy relationship with God. We become what we think, and what we meditate on, become a reality. Negative thinking, results in negative actions. Apostle Paul and Silas could have allowed the predicament of being in prison stop them, but they used resources that were effective and that were sure to bring results.

Prayer and Praise are weapons against the strategy of the enemy. King Jehoshaphat, in the book of Chronicles used prayer, praise and fasting to win the battle and God set ambushment against their enemies including Satan himself. When you learn to pray and praise your way out. Ambushment will have your enemies fighting each other. The enemies will certainly fall when you approach your battles in this manner. The effectual fervent prayer of a righteous man avails much. We are to come boldly unto the throne of Grace, that we might obtain grace and help.

God wants us to lean on him. God watches over his word to perform it. He looks for ways to bless and help his own. Prayer is power and faith with prayer is awesome. God honors faith, in fact the word says, the just shall live by faith. Stretch your faith to believe God for a hard thing. Whatever we may be facing or dealing with in life; God can work it out. He is a mighty God, and he does awesome wonders. Even though God knows what we are facing in life, he has designed us to ask him for specific needs and desires in prayer.

Luke 18:1 says *"And he spake a parable unto them to this end, that men ought to always pray and not to faint.* Fainting in the face of adversity shows how little strength one has and ultimately it shows how much faith one has. We must remember that faith is something that God honors. When you mix faith with prayer, it's no telling what miracles God will release in your life. A prayer-less person should expect very little from God and on the other hand a praying person should expect a whole lot from God. God is not happy to see you in pain or to see you lose what is dear to your heart. He wants to give you back what the Devil stole from you. Prayer is authority, knowing that demons are subject under you. We must know who we are in God. God have given us power to tread on serpents, and scorpions and nothing should by any means hurt you.

Maybe God wants to give you something better than you had. All is not lost. In fact, there's a new beginning for you. **<u>When you have a spirit of expectancy, God will do wonders</u>**. Your positive inner feelings along with your positive speech will open up many doors of blessings in your life. You can talk your way out of a situation that has backed you in the corner. Talk your way to victory, and defeat every enemy in your life.

Regardless of how things look on the right and on the left, do what seems strange – talk your way to victory. Many times people have talked so negative, so much so, until they stayed in the same ruts and actually received the negative things that came from their mouths. You must believe what you are saying until it gets in your spirit.

Use the mishaps and downfalls to come up higher in your life. Show the adversary who you are in Christ, by not giving into your situation, and by having a wholesome and healthy prayer life, along with abiding faith. God is a promise keeper and all of his promises are **<u>yea and amen</u>**!! Some people know how to use the word of God to combat problems that arise and some faint and wonder why God allowed these circumstances. Which one do you choose to do in a crisis?

There will be problems and troubles in this life, but God gave us biblical examples of how to overcome. The scripture said, *"He that over-cometh shall inherit all things."* You overcome by the blood of the lamb and the word of your testimony. Say it, "The victory is mine," and now believe it, you have the victory. Don't let circumstances dictate to you, but tell your circumstances about your God, and your circumstances will take a back seat to such powerful words of faith. Ephesians 6, *"Be strong in the Lord and in the power of his might. Put on the whole armor of God and you will be able to stand against the wiles of the Devil. For Satan walks about as a roaring lion seeking whom he may devour. He is just as a lion, he has no teeth, submit yourself to God, and resist the Devil and he will flee from you. For Satan comes but to kill, to steal, and destroy."*

Now we know what our enemy is all about. Now let's utilize what power and resources that God gave us. God have all power in his hand, and he has given us power, so there is nothing that can overtake us, if we stand in God's power and work the word of God. For God inherits the praises of his people. You want a solution to problems, start giving God the praise. That is what many bible scholars did. As stated earlier in this chapter, Jehoshaphat won a tremendous battle without having to lift a finger to fight. He set up a choir, and put them ahead of his army, and the enemies destroyed themselves.

How about facing your battles with praise to God and let God fight for us. God wants us to hold our peace and he will fight our battles. Let the praises of God go ahead of you, but not just a verbal praise with no real meanings from the heart. God is worthy to be praised. All you have to do is remember your past victories and know who he is and your heart will utter praises through your mouth and through the clapping of your hands. This is a wonderful way to defeat the Devil.

Praise God in advance, with stringed instruments. Having a heart of praise is extremely powerful because while you are praising God inwardly or outwardly God is working strong on your behalf. I've seen situations turn around immediately when I began to praise God instead of worrying and fainting in my mind about situations. I begin to think of God's goodness and remember some of the things he worked out for me, praise came from my heart and my mouth uttered the praises that belong to God. Things worked out.

And were resolved because I left my problems with the one who can fix them. Worrying won't solve the problems, so replace worry with faith, and watch God work, and watch your own spirit stay revived. It's not how much you read the word but how you let the word work for you.

Having our emotions lifted in a service is beautiful, I love a good anointed service but life is teaching me that I have to apply those words from the sermon. When the storms of life cross my path, I can do one or two things, I can work the word, and praise God and pray fervently, or I can faint in my mind and forget all the good bible promises and the beautiful words from the preacher's sermon and let my circumstances walk all over me.

God will bring his promises to your mind if you are willing to receive them. Problems will either make you or break you. They will cause you to rely and depend on God's deliverance or they will make you doubt God and have you give in to what you are facing. We serve a loving Savior, he will walk and talk with us and encourage us through our most difficult times. He will never leave you or forsake you. God wants us to pass each test that he gives us. God sends his word, knowing that things will be presented to us in our lives. He is watching to see how we will respond to things we face.

Will the word we received at the church and personal times of reading the bible be put to work or will the problems overtake us and kill our spirit. Remember Satan wants to get you discouraged so that you won't fight him. He wants you to accuse God of not being true to his word. What will we do in our times of testing and afflictions? The choice is ours.

That's where prevailing prayer comes into play; these are prayers that have been prayed before the problems ever come. That is why prayers are so powerful. Prayer wins victories and keeps you in communication with God, while gaining strength and answers to prayers. Pray and praise your way out as Paul and Silas did and won supernatural victories.

Judges 4, 5, Prophetess and Judge Deborah sang praise to god for giving Barak and her victory over Sisera. Sisera actually fled from them and ended up dying and their King Jabin of Canaan.

Chapter Ten
"God Will Bring Restoration"

Restoration is coming, just as the book of Joel says, God will restore what the locust, and canker worm and palmer worm have eaten. Knowing God is the best thing that can happen to anyone. To know God is to love him. He is a true friend. He is absolutely true to his word. After years of being without, God will give it all back to you, as if you never lost anything. It won't be any lack, even though years and months have gone by. He'll put it back right in its proper place and, in fact God will give you back more than what you lost. He's so awesome, magnificent, marvelous, mind blowing, breath taking, a head lifter and so much more, which is inexhaustible.

God's awesomeness and character never runs out. He's whatever you need him to be and still He has more. He is all powerful, all knowing and is everywhere and fills every space. What a mighty God we serve. Restore means just what it says. A return or bringing back again what was taken from you. The enemy walks in our camp and takes or steals what belongs to us, but he must let it go in Jesus name. The all powerful and almighty God is about to release your possessions, health, relationships, money, jobs, ministries, etc.

You are about to give birth to what you have inside. The closer you are to the birth of your blessings, the harder it gets. That's when Satan will try and convince us that nothing is going to happen so give up, quit, forsake your God, but don't do it. Hold on tight and push now in Jesus name. Our God have not forsaken us, he is a keeper of his promises. What God have given you in a dream or vision hold on to it and believe. Wait, it's almost there.

Hold your head up and believe your God, and watch God give you what he promised, not only will he give you what he promised but he is going to restore your lost. Some of you lost your jobs, your ministries, your joy, your peace, your anointing, your zeal, your strength and motivation, but I declare to you in the matchless name of Jesus that it's coming back seven fold. Just believe and praise him like you all ready have it. God loves praise, so praise him hallelujah!!!

Life has a way of robbing us of what God put in us. When troubles come to break your spirit, remember the word of God.

"His word will not return unto him void, but shall accomplish that which he purposes it to." "No weapon formed against you shall prosper, every tongue that shall rise up against you in judgment, thou shalt condemn." The victory belongs to the child of God, and in the name of Jesus what was stolen from you will be restored. It is hard to believe when you have waited so long and the longer you wait, the worst things seem to get, but you must not accuse God falsely because of what your enemy the devil have taken.

God don't go around breaking up relationships, at the same time he is not going to fix somethings that is not good for you or your relationship with him, but God will give you better than what you had. It's time for supernatural miracles and blessings in the lives of the believers. Open your heart to receive the miracles he promised. The word has been spoken and declared and the word promises for our prayers to be answered. You won't have to pray about this no more. It's your time child of God lift up your head and walk into your blessings, healing, deliverances, and miracles. Take your blessings and don't throw them away, don't' give up on them; they are right at the door. If you can conceive them in your mind, heart, you can have them. See yourself with your prayers answered.

See your new job, healings and new relationships. Faith says I can have it, worry says I don't believe I'll get it. This is the end time and blessing are being released on God's people, new homes, cars, marriages, children, ministries, are about to come to pass. The manifestations of these and other blessings have all ready been released in the lives of God's people. I have witnessed in my own life how God is restoring what the enemy took from me. Each day I feel more and more whole again. My mind and strength is renewed. My hope has come alive again. I am conceiving in my spirit what God is doing and about to do in my life and in the lives of God's people.

Great things was stolen from me and Satan's desire was for me to completely turn my back on God but instead of me turning my back on God, I got closer to God and little by little I seen my life reshaping into a much better life than I had before. God restores to the point where you feel you've never lost a thing. He'll make your life so much better until you will be thankful that you had a lost. If you had not experienced the lost, you would not be able to experience the restoration.

A supernatural restoration, second to none that only God can give is on the way. As David said in Psalms 51, "restore unto me the joy of thy salvation." Thankfully my joy was restored after suffering great lost. Life is different now but I am much better than before. "He restored my Soul" Psalms 23